D0378821

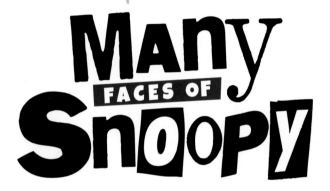

Many
FACES OF
Snoopy

CHARLES M. SCHULZ

Andrews McMeel
Publishing®

a division of Andrews McMeel Universal

JOE COOL

Joe Cool is king of the college campus.
He's calm, obviously cool, and loves hanging out.
The hardest he ever works is when he's
ordering pizza.

JOE PREPPY

The stylish and dapper Joe Preppy—in his sport coat, bowtie, and glasses—is quite dashing and always in fashion. He is ready for any occasion.

FLYING ACE

The Flying Ace soars high above the clouds in his Sopwith Camel, keeping watch for his archenemy, the Red Baron. When he's not on a high-flying adventure you may find him in a café quaffing root beers with friends and mesdemoiselles.

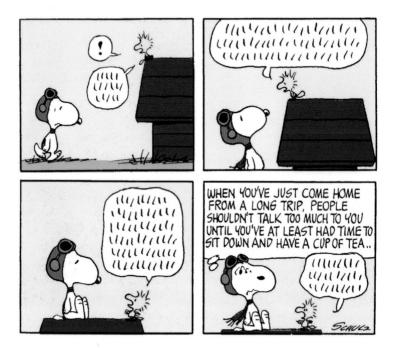

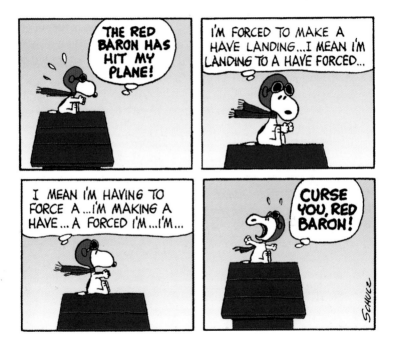

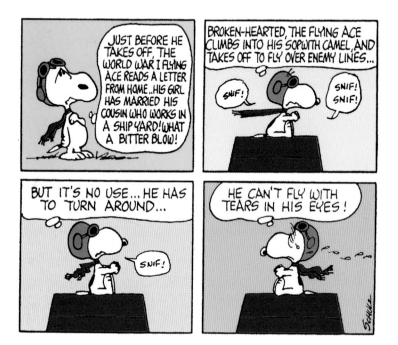

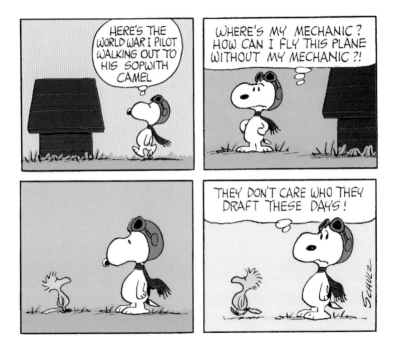

SECRET AGENT

There is intrigue everywhere, but the sly
Secret Agent will uncover the truth, no matter what.
He is always on the case.

BEAGLE
SCOUT

A Beagle Scout looks at the planet with a sense of
wonder and adventure. He is always ready to camp,
explore new trails, and experience the many joys
of the great outdoors with his buddies.

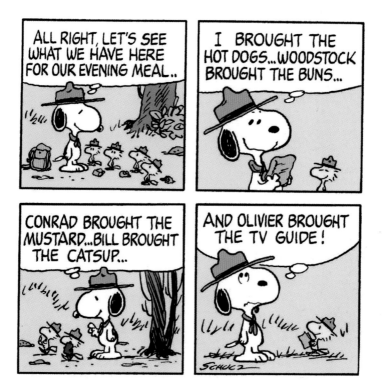

MASKED MARVEL

The Masked Marvel is strong, brave, and loves a good arm-wrestling tournament. His clever disguise keeps his true identity a secret.

FLASHBEAGLE

Snoopy loves to dance. His "Happy Dance"
is legendary but he's not above grooving to
newer dance crazes too. As Flashbeagle,
Snoopy doesn't need sequins to sparkle onstage,
just his headband and sweatshirt.

FIERCE PIRATE

The Fierce Pirate fears nothing, thirsts for excitement, and is a master of the high seas. Don't let the name fool you though; he's not really fierce, he just likes to tell tall tales.

Peanuts is distributed internationally by Universal Uclick.

Many Faces of Snoopy

Andrews McMeel Publishing
a division of Andrews McMeel Universal
1130 Walnut Street, Kansas City, Missouri 64106

www.andrewsmcmeel.com

16 17 18 19 20 TEN 10 9 8 7 6 5 4 3 2 1

ISBN: 978-1-4494-7888-9

Library of Congress Control Number: 2015957287

Attention: Schools and Businesses

Andrews McMeel books are available at quantity discounts with bulk purchase for educational, business, or sales promotional use. For information, please e-mail the Andrews McMeel Publishing Special Sales Department: specialsales@amuniversal.com.